ACKNOWLEDGMENTS

A book like this doesn't grow out of a vacuum. It emerges from a vast, scattered community of people with one great thing in common: They love animals.

Thank you, Petco, for allowing us access to your stores, and especially Steve Watson from the Lakewood store, who was unfailingly tolerant and often fun. Thanks to Reptiles Unlimited and Paw Shoppe Pet Center, both of Long Beach. Several of Thoresen Pape's animals rise from these pages, in no small part due to Thor's skill at creating interesting backdrops. Thanks also to Amia Kurs for assisting on several photo shoots.

So many people opened their doors to us, sharing their time and pets. Everywhere we found beautiful, well cared for animals. Most heartwarming was to discover a vast army of unassuming, unsung heroes who regularly devote much of their free time to rescuing needy animals. Thanks to Caroline Charland and the folks at Bunny Bunch, SPCALA, the Pet Assistance Foundation, the Southern California Association for Miniature Potbellied Pigs, and all the other animal rescue groups and foundations that helped in the development of this book.

Thanks to pet owners and/or breeders John Zappe, Bob and Jill McFall, Mo and Elaine Feinblatt, Judy Hernandez, Raquel Correa, Kathy Lawson, Nick Orchard, Jessica Hill, Shelly Hamagishi, Kevin Griffin, Renae and David Henry, Joe Mansfield, Angela Barela, Bill and Betty Herman, Cynthia L. Taylor, Joe and Anne Urcis, and Tina Tramonto.

Special thanks to Art Hernandez, who made my containment box "photo studio," to Kenny Lanza for constructing my camera mounting rig, and to everyone at Jet Abrasives for doing their jobs so well as to allow me to mess around in 3-D.

Phantom3D® is a registered trademark of Barry Rothstein.
Produced under license from Owen C. Western, U.S. Pat. No. 6,389,236.
All phantogram 3D materials produced in cooperation with Aubrey Imaging, San Jose, California:
Exclusive Licensor of phantogram and OpUp™ 3D Technology under U.S. Pat. No. 6,614,427.

Front cover (dog) and title page photo: image100/SuperStock. Front cover (cat) photo: Dreamstime.com/Isselee.

Book design by Amy E. Achaibou.
Typeset in Gotham, Chalet, and Rockwell.
Manufactured in China.

Library of Congress Cataloging-in-Publication Data
Rothstein, Barry.
Eye-popping 3-D pets : phantogram animals you can practically pet! / by Barry Rothstein and Betsy Rothstein.
p. cm.
Accompanied by red-and-blue 3-D glasses.
ISBN 978-0-8118-6257-8
1. Pets—Pictorial works—Juvenile literature. 2. Pets—Juvenile literature.
3. Photography, Stereoscopic—Juvenile literature. 4. Toy and movable books—Specimens.
I. Rothstein, Betsy. II. Title. III. Title: Three-dimensional pets.
SF416.5.R68 2009
636.088'7—dc22
2008052604

10 9 8 7 6 5 4 3 2 1

Chronicle Books LLC
680 Second Street, San Francisco, California 94107
www.chroniclekids.com

EYE-POPPING
3-D PETS

PHANTOGRAM ANIMALS YOU CAN PRACTICALLY PET!

By Barry Rothstein and Betsy Rothstein

chronicle books · san francisco

Contents

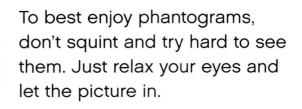

To best enjoy phantograms, don't squint and try hard to see them. Just relax your eyes and let the picture in.

Welcome to the World of Phantogram Pets!

You've opened not just a book but a world of 28 animals that you can practically touch! That's the magic of phantograms—they go beyond the effects of traditional three-dimensional photography. The images appear to rise off the page, so you see a "phantom" animal that's just begging to be petted! Many of the animal photos are even life-size, adding to the *"Wow! Is it really there?"* effect.

As you make your way through this book, you'll find facts about the pets and information about taking care of them. You'll find out which pets are up all night, which one can be taught to play a toy piano, which one steals car keys, and which ones dine on canned crickets!

Along with each pet, you'll see phantogram toys, foods, perches, aquarium decor, and more. You'll get a sense of what it would be like to own each animal. And hey, who knows? Maybe you'll find a pet you would actually like to have in your home with you. In the meantime, enjoy your phantogram friends!

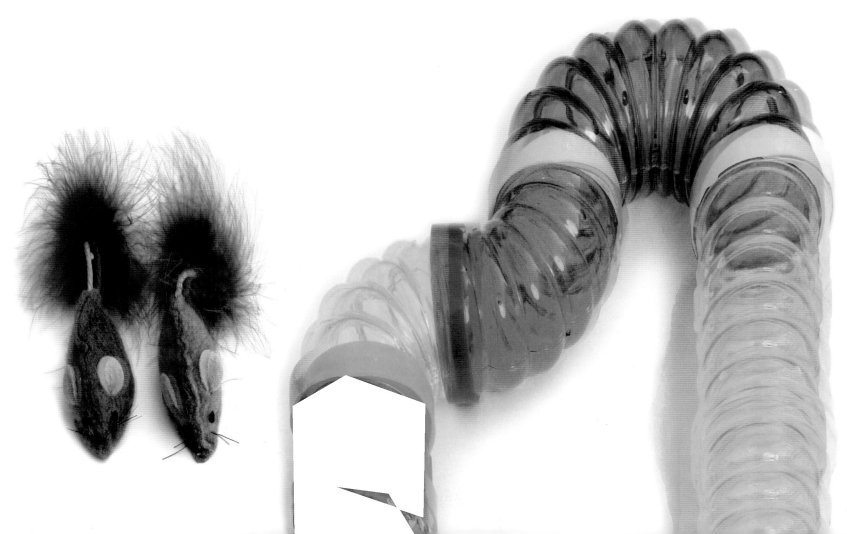

How 3-D Works

3-D is ordinary stuff. You see in 3-D every day, from your first waking moment until you close your eyes to go to sleep at night. You might even see in 3-D in your dreams. But probably you don't think much about it until you go to a 3-D movie or look at a 3-D book. So what is 3-D?

The One-Eye Test

Hold one hand over one of your eyes. Walk around the room, and with your other hand reach out and touch objects on a tabletop and on the walls. Try to touch the objects lightly, barely skimming them with your fingertips. Now do the same thing with both eyes open. Do you notice that it's harder to sense how far away things are when you're looking with only one eye? With only one eye, do you notice that sometimes you will reach for something and find that it's a little farther away than you thought?

With only one eye, you can't see in 3-D. You can see clearly, but you aren't seeing depth the way you can when you look with two eyes.

Two Eyes, Two Views

Your eyes are like cameras—not just one camera but two of them— that are constantly taking pictures, but not exactly the same pictures. Your eyes are spaced about 2 inches (5 centimeters) apart, so the pictures your right eye takes are a little bit different from the pictures your left eye takes. Your brain compares

the two pictures and puts the information together for you. Instead of seeing the world only as an ordinary photograph, two-dimensionally (in length and width), you also see the third dimension, depth.

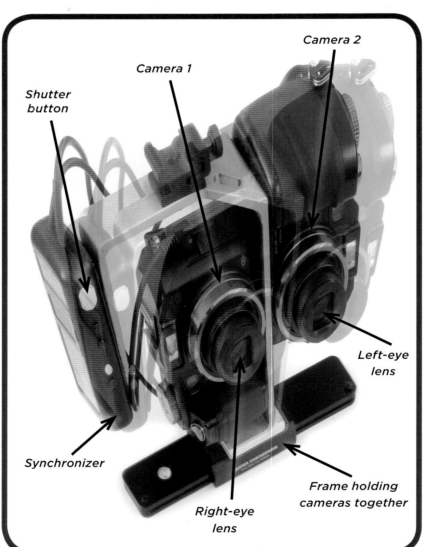

Shutter button

Camera 1

Camera 2

Left-eye lens

Synchronizer

Right-eye lens

Frame holding cameras together

The Magic of Phantograms

The 3-D pictures in this book are phantograms, a new kind of 3-D photography. All 3-D images show depth, but phantograms go a step further: They try to imitate normal vision very precisely. In this book, we reproduce the real world on paper, attempting to give your eyes exactly the same visual experience they'd have if the animals and toys on the page were really there in front of you. They should rise magically from the page. They should seem real!

To make these animal phantograms, we used a special camera setup: two cameras mounted together with a single shutter button on a synchronizer (which makes the cameras work in unison). The device takes two pictures at once, one for your left eye and one for your right eye.

Putting the Images Together

After the images are captured, we use photo software to combine the two images so they can be viewed with red-and-blue 3-D glasses. Here's how it works:

Left-eye image

Right-eye image

Left-eye image turns blue.

Right-eye image turns red.

Put on your glasses and look at the two images with one eye closed. Do you notice how the red image fades away when you look at it through the red lens? A similar thing happens with the blue image and the blue lens. This color filtering means that each eye is going to see a different image when the images are combined in the next step.

When you look at the combined images without your glasses, what you see looks like a blurry mess. With your 3-D glasses on, though, your left eye sees the left-eye image, and your right eye sees the right-eye image, thanks to the color filtering. That's how an image on paper becomes three-dimensional!

The images are placed on top of each other.

Dogs

How did dogs, the relatives of wolves, become "man's best friend"? According to the most popular theory, the wolves made the first move. Picture a clan of early humans—the men would return from hunting, and everyone would have a feast. Clever wolves realized that plenty of scraps would remain after such a feast, so they started hanging around the humans' settlements. As those wolves had pups, those pups became even more comfortable with humans. Over several generations, these wolves became the first pet dogs.

Big Dog, Little Dog

If dogs are descended from wolves, how did we get so many different kinds of dogs? The answer, in two words, is *selective breeding*. In other words, a breeder selects, or chooses, two dogs with appealing traits and combines those traits in one dog.

One Scotsman, Lord Tweedmouth, wanted a dog that loved to swim as much as a Tweed water spaniel but was bigger and smart and gentle enough to retrieve. He bred his water spaniel, Belle, with Nous, the only yellow puppy in a litter of black wavy-haired retrievers. By breeding Belle and Nous's yellow pups with more and more other breeds, Tweedmouth came closer and closer to the combination he was looking for until—ta-dah!—he created what we now know as a golden retriever.

Doggie Duties

If they lived in the wild, dogs would travel miles a day with their packs. Pet dogs don't have to travel miles a day, but they still need exercise. So if you want to own a dog, you'll need to take it for walks every day. How long you walk and how often depends on the size and energy level of your dog. For a very high-energy dog, you can even add a doggie backpack to make the walks more demanding. No matter what kind of dog you have, exercise is the key to having a dog that is calm and happy at home.

You'll also need to teach your dog discipline, which might mean working with a trainer. You can't have your retriever jumping up on an elderly aunt as she comes through the door! Even with exercise and discipline, your work is not done. You'll need to feed your dog regularly, too. A puppy needs to eat several times a day because its tiny tummy can hold only so much food. You'll also need to give your dog plenty of fresh water. Then, after food, comes poop—yet another job, as you will have to pick it up to keep your yard or neighborhood clean.

Dogs enjoy chewing on knotted rope toys like this, and many enjoy playing "tug" with the rope if their owner holds one end.

The Fun Part

Dogs are great at watching your actions and learning from you, so teach your dog plenty of tricks. It's good for the dog because it helps with discipline. It's also fun for both of you. After the work and the training are done, you can give your puppy all the affection you want—it's the best reward, for your dog and for you!

Boomer *is a miniature dachshund. The dachshund was originally bred to hunt badgers, animals that burrow underground. Because of its long body, the dachshund can squeeze into narrow tunnels. Boomer loves chasing squirrels, so his owner has to hold him tight by the leash when they go on walks.*

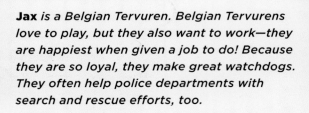

Jax is a Belgian Tervuren. Belgian Tervurens love to play, but they also want to work—they are happiest when given a job to do! Because they are so loyal, they make great watchdogs. They often help police departments with search and rescue efforts, too.

A pug's wrinkled face may look serious, but the pug is a fun-loving dog. Pugs love interacting with people, and they are happy to sleep in your lap all day. **Corey** knows how to balance on his hind legs, and his favorite place is the beach.

Australian shepherds, also called Aussies, are not from Australia! They were bred in the United States and named after the sheepherders they worked with, who had come from Australia. Aussies are intelligent, and they are one of the best family dogs. They love to play, but they're perfectly content being couch potatoes, too!

April *is a West Highland white terrier (also known as a Westie), and she loves to hunt. That's not surprising: Westies were bred in Scotland to hunt small animals. April chases squirrels and chipmunks, and she loves to bob for apples in a small swimming pool.*

Diamond is a Chihuahua, a dog known for its high energy—and major attitude! Chihuahuas may be the smallest dog breed in the world, but they don't act small. In fact, they often bark fearlessly at much larger dogs. Chihuahuas are fond of sleeping under blankets and hiding in cozy places, so Chihuahua owners have to watch where they sit!

Jack Russell terriers were originally bred to hunt foxes—they'll even follow an animal deep underground. A Jack Russell terrier needs a lot of space to play in, like a big backyard or a dog park where it can run free.

19

Cats

Ever since humans began farming, cats have hung around, feeding on the mice and rats that raided the farmers' stored food. Obviously, this was a good thing! People eventually gave in to the charm of cats and invited them into their homes.

Social Skills

For cats to be thoroughly tame, they need human contact before they're 3 weeks old. Interaction with other cats is also important until at least 12 weeks of age. Consider adopting sibling kittens or a mother and daughter. Even an older male cat can play a parental role, grooming and play-fighting with a new kitten.

Kittens love to play, and playing is about more than just having fun. Playing helps kittens develop important social skills and physical coordination. Give your kitten cat toys to bat around and chew, and be sure to play with your kitten several times a day, especially if your kitten does not have a fellow feline companion.

Dawn and Dusk Hunters

Cats like to be active at dawn and again at dusk. That means they're *crepuscular*, not *nocturnal*. Dawn and dusk are the times when they would hunt in the wild.

If you start finding "presents"—dead mice and other prey—in the house, you'll know that your cat is making use of its superb hunting skills. Our amazing feline friends can run up to 31 miles (50 kilometers) per hour and use their fangs to snag their prey. They can fit through holes no bigger than their head (having a floating collarbone helps), which allows them to sneak into small spaces.

Playful Predators

Cats' predatory instincts (their natural tendencies to hunt) make them great playmates. Their eyesight is very sensitive to movement, so they'll stalk and pounce on any string or cat toy you wiggle in front of them. Cats especially love toys stuffed with catnip, an herb they adore. Toys stuffed with the dried plant will cause a cat to roll around, leap about, purr, and drool. You can grow your own catnip to give your kitty a treat.

Want a Cat?

Perfectly capable of surviving on their own, cats are smart enough to know when they've got it good: food they don't have to hunt, a warm place to sleep, and a faithful human to meet their every need. If being a cat's servant seems a fair trade for a little play and petting, a cat may be the perfect animal for you. And hey, you'll have a resident rodent exterminator, too, should you need one!

Soft toys with feathers provide great entertainment and stimulation for cats. Cats treat the toys like prey, and feathers are reminiscent of birds, which cats love to hunt.

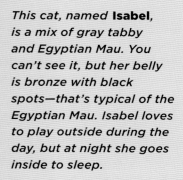

This cat, named **Isabel**, is a mix of gray tabby and Egyptian Mau. You can't see it, but her belly is bronze with black spots—that's typical of the Egyptian Mau. Isabel loves to play outside during the day, but at night she goes inside to sleep.

This silver tabby American shorthair is ready for her dinner! ("Tabby" refers to the striping pattern of the fur.) American shorthair cats are low-maintenance, gentle, and playful. They get along well with children and dogs, but they are natural hunters, so keep small pets away!

This kitten is a Persian, a long-haired breed that is believed to have originated in Persia. She has the tiny flat nose and huge eyes that are typical of the breed. She'll grow into an adult with a small body and short legs. Persians are known to be especially sweet-tempered cats.

Guinea Pigs

Guinea pigs can thank sailors for their popularity: The first people to keep guinea pigs as pets were sailors—they brought them to Europe from South America. These rodents may have been named after Guiana, a region of South America (which was perhaps confused with Guinea, in Africa, a name sometimes given to any unknown, faraway country). The little animals were called pigs because of the squeaking, piglike noises they make.

Friends to All

Guinea pigs have been bred over many generations to show particular traits and to create many different breeds. Although guinea pigs can be nervous, they're basically friendly, nosy little characters. The fact that they rarely bite—even when scared—makes them a great pet for young children.

Read My Body Signals

Like all animals, guinea pigs have nonverbal ways of communicating. For example, squeaking can mean the guinea pig is feeling pain, fear, or loneliness—or is just begging for food. When guinea pigs touch each other on the nose, they may be checking for illness or simply greeting each other. Jumping shows happiness, and cooing is a calming or reassuring sound. Guinea pigs will turn rigid and play dead when threatened by an enemy.

Guinea Pig Basics

Because they do best in pairs, if you want a guinea pig, get two. Before bringing a guinea pig home, you'll

These "popcorn sticks" are a great chewy treat for guinea pigs. They're made of a variety of puffed grains and seeds, so guinea pigs can gnaw and snack at the same time. The green grips allow them to attach to a cage.

need a big, sturdy cage. Because guinea pigs are by no means escape artists, the cage can be open at the top. You'll also need litter to cover the cage floor, a food dish, and a hanging water bottle (which keeps water fresher than a water bowl).

Hidey-Holes and Chew Toys

Guinea pigs like to have a "hidey-hole"— a place where they can chill out when they're overstimulated, and a place where they can feel safe when they sleep. Pet stores sell all sorts of hidey-holes, but an overturned bowl or box or even a paper bag will do.

Guinea pigs also love balls and chew toys. Give them wood blocks or crumpled paper, and they'll gnaw and shred to their heart's content.

Cuddly Buds

One big thing your guinea pigs will need from you, besides a daily check on their food and water supply, is a once-a-week cage cleaning. That may sound like a lot of work, but remember: These guys are soft, cuddly, curious, and friendly, and they don't bite. That's a pretty good return on an investment in daily meals and once-a-week chores!

These two guinea pig pals have beautiful, three-colored coats. The small wreath-like willow chew ring in the picture is one item they can gnaw on to keep their teeth trim. For fun, they like to push around little plastic balls like the one shown here.

Hamsters

If you've ever met a hamster, it was probably a Syrian (golden) hamster. This hamster comes from Syria, in the Middle East, where it lives in burrows in the desert. Syrian hamsters were first bred and studied by zoologists in the 1930s, and since then, these little furry rodents have become one of the world's most popular pets.

Power Pouches

The name *hamster* comes from the German word *hamstern*, which means "to hoard" (to save large quantities of stuff). Spend a little time with a hamster, and you'll find out why. This little hoarder has pockets on either side of its mouth that extend down the sides of its neck.

In the wild, hamsters stuff their cheeks with food and then return to their home to store it. Though they don't need to, hamsters may carry their food to another spot in their cage, eat some of it there, and bury the rest.

Mother hamsters have another very important use for these pouches. If a mother senses danger to her young, she will stuff her babies into her pouches and take them back to her nest.

Gnawing Is Nice

Hamsters have very sharp teeth that grow constantly. To keep their teeth trim, they need to gnaw regularly, so they need plenty of wood chews.

Because of their habit of gnawing, hamsters need a strong cage, one made of metal, not wood or cardboard. These little guys *are* escape artists, and once free, they are rarely found. Not only can they get lost in hard-to-access spaces (like your walls), but they might also gnaw on electric wires, an activity that is dangerous for them and definitely not good for your home!

A plastic tube like this can be attached to a hamster's cage, giving a hamster a place to crawl. As hamsters are burrowers in the wild, running through narrow tunnels is natural for them.

So, If You'd Like to House a Hamster . . .

Be ready to handle your hamster daily, change its water, give it fresh food, and clean the cage regularly. Hamsters love to be touched and stay healthiest when they receive lots of attention. A hamster can learn to recognize its name and come when you call it, so calling it by its name is one way you can interact with your hamster!

Oh, and hamsters are nocturnal—they like to burrow, gnaw, and run on their wheels at night, so you might want to keep your hamster's cage out of your bedroom if you won't be able to sleep through your hamster's nighttime activities!

If you love speed, Roborovski hamsters may be the breed for you: They are the fastest hamsters! In the wild, hamsters can run miles every night in search of food. With an exercise wheel like the one shown here, pet hamsters can get that kind of exercise without ever leaving their cage.

Ferrets

Curious, hyper, playful—all these words describe the popular pet ferret. The word *ferret* seems to have come from the Latin *furittus*, meaning "little fur thief." *Thief* is the key word here. As you read about ferrets, see if you can figure out how they earned their name.

Party Animals

Ferrets play hard and sleep hard. They love to chase, wrestle, and pounce. It's quite common for these comical klutzes to run into things and trip over their own feet as they play.

When a ferret wants its human or another ferret to roughhouse, it'll do a "weasel war dance": It'll make its body rigid and then thrash its head back and forth. With its jaw wide open, it'll hop backward or sideways. Its fur stands on end, and it pants, almost as if it were laughing. The crazy dance doesn't stop until the ferret's buddy takes the bait and tussles with it.

Hidey-Holes

Ferrets are also famous for stashing small items in hidey-holes. Ferret owners have found socks, calculators, car keys, video-game controllers, and even bags of onions hidden away by their sneaky pets!

Curious Creatures

Ferrets are so curious and fearless that they often put themselves at risk. They're fascinated by small spaces and love to go down holes. Because of this fascination, hunters have used ferrets to chase rabbits out of their holes. Ferrets have also helped electricians pull wires through underground tubes. As you can imagine, an animal that enjoys going on such adventures can be a challenge to keep as a pet!

Are You Fit for a Ferret?

Your ferret will need a secure cage to sleep in and to stay in when you can't watch it. A leash will keep it safely near you (especially outside). And your home will have to be ferret-proofed—there can be no small holes or crevices that a ferret might squeeze into.

Being very energetic, ferrets need to leave their cages for at least 4 hours every day so they can get the exercise they need. And that out-of-cage time has to be carefully supervised, or your ferret might go missing. Fortunately for ferret owners, there is time off: Ferrets sleep 16 to 18 hours a day. They tend to be active at dusk and dawn, so be prepared for an early wake-up call!

Ferrets love to play with toys. Balls like these with bells inside are a perfect choice, as the sound adds extra stimulation.

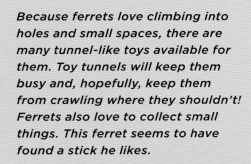

Because ferrets love climbing into holes and small spaces, there are many tunnel-like toys available for them. Toy tunnels will keep them busy and, hopefully, keep them from crawling where they shouldn't! Ferrets also love to collect small things. This ferret seems to have found a stick he likes.

Rabbits

Rabbits were originally kept by families as a source of food, but in the late 1800s, they became popular as pets. With their gentle nature, rabbits are considered a good pet for children, as they will not usually bite when picked up. They can live outdoors in a safe enclosure that's protected from the elements (and from predators!), or they can be housetrained to live inside like a cat or dog. There are more than 200 breeds to choose from, including one called the "lionhead" that has a lion-like mane!

Busy Bunnies

In the wild, rabbits are very social and have a *lot* of babies. A female can have several litters a year, each with 6 to 9 young, typically. The world's largest recorded litter consisted of 24 babies!

Rabbits are entirely herbivorous (they eat only plants), and they are crepuscular, meaning they are most active in the early morning and early evening, although sometimes they are active throughout the night—kind of the opposite of us humans!

Many rabbits burrow underground for shelter and protection, using their claws to do the digging.

Run, Rabbit, Run!

Rabbits have powerful hind legs and are great at maneuvering on the run. Have you ever seen a rabbit running in the wild? It's not only fast but agile, weaving back and forth—the rabbit is a challenge even to the fastest coyote. Plus, the position of its eyes allows it to see behind itself without turning its head. A lot of teachers would like to have that ability!

Pinecones are a great natural chew for rabbits.

Social Animal

Being highly social, pet rabbits love to be around their humans. In the wild, the dwellings of burrowing rabbits are called warrens, which are underground cities. As many as 100 rabbits can be found in one warren. Rabbits in a warren will nibble and lick one another to show affection. A pet rabbit that is feeling affectionate will nibble and lick its owner, too!

Bunny Basics

If you plan to keep your rabbit outside, you'll need a hutch to keep it safe. A hutch is a pen or cage, usually made of wood, with a screened window and a door. It is lined with hay because rabbits like to gnaw—bits of wood and hay are good for them to chew on. The hutch should be kept off the ground so that other wild animals don't frighten your rabbit.

If you keep your rabbit indoors, you'll need to rabbit-proof your home. Hide any electric cords, and be sure your rabbit doesn't chew the carpet.

Is a Bunny a Good Bet?

You do the math! A little cage cleaning once a week plus regular food and water deliveries equals a fuzzy buddy to cuddle. And it'll eat your veggies for you!

A rabbit's food usually consists of feed pellets, shown here in the small bowl, along with fresh salad veggies and very small amounts of barley or oats. This rabbit has a chew toy, seen leaning against the food bowl, that is meant to resemble a carrot.

Potbellied Pigs

The potbellied pig became popular in the mid-1980s as an exotic pet. Although a potbellied pig is easy to train, anyone thinking about adopting one had better be ready to share space in a big way. A piglet is about the size of a puppy, but an adult may be the size of a large dog and weigh as much as 200 pounds (90 kilograms)!

Pig Training

Pigs are very intelligent animals. With such active minds, they get bored easily and will chew on wallpaper, dig up linoleum flooring, tip over tables, and even open refrigerators. Training is one way to keep boredom at bay. Potbellied pigs are easily trained to do tricks, like shaking "hands" or even playing a toy piano.

How do you teach a pig to play piano? With lots of patience! First, put small treats on the keys of a toy piano. When the pig accidentally dings a key with its snout, praise it. In time, you can give the treat after the pig plays a single key and then after it plays a series of keys.

Pig Love

Pigs are highly affectionate. They love having their bellies rubbed and their bristly skin scratched. Being social herd animals, pigs like to remain close to other creatures; pet pigs will often sleep on their human's feet. If kept outside, your pet is much better off with another pig for company than it is alone.

This bowl of healthy "pig food" contains broccoli and carrots. Pigs often eat out of dog dishes like this one.

Pig Out

Being omnivores, potbellied pigs eat everything: fruit, vegetables, grains, and meat. They will dig up tasty roots and graze on grass, clover, and dandelions. Like most humans, pigs will eat any sweet, fatty food that's available. They'll also eat their vegetables, but only when nothing else is around. Pigs need water not only for drinking but also for cooling off. Because pigs do not sweat or pant, they need a pool to bathe in or a cool, muddy spot in the yard to lie in.

Pig Reality Check

Small children and pigs don't mix, as a pig may try to push toddlers around to show them who's boss. Likewise, dogs aren't good pig companions: Dogs' predator instincts come out around prey animals—and that includes pigs.

If you don't have a yard, a pig is probably not for you. Remember: Your adorable piglet will become the size of a piece of furniture! A yard will give you (and your pig!) the space you need to feel comfortable. If your pig is going to sleep inside, it'll need its own space, ideally a room of its own. However, your affectionate, clever friend will make your efforts well worth your while.

The Vietnamese potbellied pig is black, white, or black-and-white. This one, named **Hamlet**, loves to have his belly rubbed. He knows his name, and he will eat almost anything. He once started to eat one of his owner's books!

Parakeets

What most people consider a parakeet is actually a budgerigar ("budgie") parakeet, a small parrot that's native to Australia. The first budgies were brought to Europe in 1840, and since then, they have become very popular pets. They're sought after for their good looks (plenty of bright colors!) and their ability to mimic words and sounds. With help from a skilled teacher, a budgie can build a vocabulary of more than 500 words!

Budgie Beauties

There's lots of eye candy from which to choose when shopping for a budgie, as the birds come in many beautiful colors. But budgies are not all about their looks. They also make a huge variety of sounds. With chirps, trills, warbles, and angry ack-ack-acks, budgies have no problem expressing themselves. When it comes to learning human speech, males are easier to train than females. As with any training of pets, the younger, the better.

Budgies also delight in "dancing" (bobbing the head up and down). A male will do his dance for a female, but most budgies enjoy music and will dance to it!

Are You a Birdbrain?

If you choose to adopt a budgie, you will need a cage big enough for it to fly from perch to perch. Water for drinking and bathing must be changed regularly. Water and food bowls should be cleaned with hot soapy water and the cage floor cleaned regularly.

A lone parakeet in particular needs toys, especially mirrors, which give it the illusion of having a buddy. Cuttlebone, made from the shell or bone of cuttlefishes, will give your parakeet the calcium it needs, aid in digestion, and keep its bill trim.

Budgie Buddy

Once tamed, your budgie can spend time outside the cage with you. Regular "flying time" will keep your budgie exercised and healthy. You could also set up a "gym" outside the cage, equipped with swings, climbing perches, and toys.

Millet, a cereal grain, is a popular and healthy bird food. Budgies and many other birds enjoy nibbling on the seeds as a special treat.

Plan on spending as much time working with your budgie as possible, especially if it's the only bird you have. Put the care time in, and your budgie buddy will more than repay you with affection and comic entertainment.

Budgies in nature are primarily green, like these birds, but they have been bred in more than 100 colors and color combinations, including blues, yellows, violet, grays, and white.

Parrots

Parrot is the common name for a group of 360 species of birds, including parakeets and cockatoos. For centuries, parrots have attracted lots of human interest with their brilliant coloring and unique voices. They were tamed to serve not just as companions but also as status symbols, prized in ancient Rome and in the courts of Europe for centuries after.

Ahoy, Matey!

Parrots have long been associated with pirates, maybe because they were bought and sold by pirates centuries ago. Parrots were so much in demand that Christopher Columbus and later Spanish explorers were searching not only for a passage to the East Indies but also for parrots, because they believed the birds promised great riches.

Big Talkers

African gray parrots are said to be the best talkers of the parrot family. With scary accuracy, these birds will imitate a phone ringing, their owner speaking or laughing, or even a microwave oven beeping or a touch-tone phone being dialed. The Amazon parrot is said to run a close second to the African gray in its ability to speak.

Feathered Toddlers

Parrots can be like mischievous children, unlocking their cages and even taking them apart. In fact, all parrots are comparable to toddlers in intelligence. They need plenty of challenging toys to keep them occupied, or they'll get bored. One breeder keeps her parrots busy untying knots in a length of rope.

Tricky Parrots

With a good teacher (that's you!) and some tasty rewards, a parrot can learn to do all sorts of tricks. Start with a simple task like having the parrot come to you. Just hold a treat and say, "Come here." If the bird moves toward you, say "Good" and give him the treat. Each time, wait longer, encouraging the bird to come right to your hand. Later, you can teach your bird to give kisses, shake hands, and even use a little bicycle!

Want a Parrot?

Parrots live a long time—some as long as 50 or 60 years. Their lifespan is an important factor to consider. Many parrots become homeless because their owners were unprepared to care for them their whole lives. It's also important to keep in mind that parrots need outside-the-cage time. Parrots crave closeness with their "flock"—which means you and your family. Another consideration: Many parrots have piercing calls they use to locate their flock in the wild, so imagine how popular a bored, lonely parrot would be with your neighbors!

Parrots enjoy tugging and chewing on straw balls like this.

Bubo is a bronze-winged pionus parrot. Pionus parrots are generally known to be quieter than most other parrot species, often called good "apartment birds," meaning they won't disturb the neighbors so much! Shy at first, they come to love having their head, neck, and ears scratched.

Zebra Finches

Being from Australia, zebra finches might understand you if you hail them with "G'day, mate!" Zebra finches are named for the black-and-white stripes that often mark their neck. Female zebra finches, called hens, have an orange beak. The males' beaks tend to be red, and they have orange patches on their cheeks. Zebra finches have become popular pets because they breed fast and often, so there are lots of them around!

Fun Finch Facts

Two things make zebra finches fun pets: their beautiful coloring and their vocalizations, meaning their songs and calls. Although they are common birds, their coloring is fairly exotic, with a bright orange beak and cheek and black-and-white striping on the neck. In general, finches make a pleasant soft chirping. Their call is a loud beep, like that of a touch-tone phone.

On the other hand, zebra finches are not cuddly pets. Although they are social with other birds, with humans they are shy, and they don't especially like being petted and held.

Bird Buddies

It's common to keep at least two finches because they like each other's company, and it's probably most common to keep one male and one female. A male and female, if they bond, will display certain signs of their bond: They may groom each other, cuddle when they sleep, perform courtship rituals, and nest together. When a male courts a female, he sings to her, wiggles his beak, and turns his body back and forth. If you don't want baby birds, you'd better get two finches of the same sex!

The World's Weirdest

Probably the oddest zebra finch is one rare naturally born bird that developed as a male *and* a female. This incredible bird has the colorful plumage (feathers and coloring) of a male on one side and the plainer plumage of a female on the other. He-she has been very useful to scientists researching hormones and their relationship to brain development. Even birdbrains have something to interest scientists!

Fancy a Zebra Finch?

Like any pet bird, zebra finches need their cage cleaned, their water changed daily, and regular feedings of seed mix and cuttlebone for calcium. Zebras are well worth the work. Even though they aren't lovey-dovey, if you like birdsongs, they will delight your ears.

A premade nest like this can be purchased for pet birds. Zebra finches will accept almost any kind of nest to sleep in, and will even nest in a food dish if a nest is not provided!

A female zebra finch perches on top of a bar while a male zebra finch (notice his orange cheek patches) sits below her. The egg-filled nest you can see at the bottom is the covered nest style that zebra finches prefer.

Goldfish

About a thousand years ago, the Chinese took wild carp of a dull olive color and kept them in their rice paddies for food. Babies born with unusual colors were bred as pets. Those "living jewels" were exported to Europe and the United States and have become the most common pet fish in the world. Even former U.S. president Ronald Reagan had a pet goldfish while he was in the White House.

Not Just Gold

The most common type of goldfish is small, sleek, and light orange. But goldfish come in a dazzling array of colors and sizes. Goldfish produce pigment, and their coloring changes in response to light (just as some people get tans when they go out in the sun). Goldfish can lose much of their color if they're left in the dark for a long time.

The Talented Mr. Goldfish

Goldfish are smarter than you might think. They can learn to recognize individual humans and respond to their voices. The goldfish trainer Dean Pomerleau has trained his goldfish, Albert Einstein, to swim through hoops and even push a tiny soccer ball into a net! Goldfish and other pet fish have been shown to have good effects on their human owners, too—one study showed that people felt more relaxed after watching fish swim!

Room to Grow

Goldfish can grow to 8 inches (20 centimeters) or more in length if they have enough room. A big tank with at least 10 gallons (38 liters) of water per fish is the best bet; otherwise the oxygen supply will be limited. (Through their gills, fish absorb the dissolved oxygen in water.)

A Golden Opportunity for You?

Although goldfish are relatively easy to take care of—no shedding and no walks in the rain!—they do require regular care. Goldfish will eat and eat until their intestines explode, so feed them only once a day. Also, it is important to remember that goldfish (like all fish) should not be touched. Touching fish can damage their protective coating and expose them to harmful bacteria.

Keep your fish tank clean and feed your guy regularly, and you may be enjoying your goldfish for years to come. And that might be many years: Although most household goldfish live no more than 10 years, goldfish have been known to live 20 years or more—even as long as 45 years!

Decorating your aquarium is part of the fun of owning fish. Sculpted castles like this are among the many "furnishings" available.

Goldfish are cold-water fish, which means they don't need a heated aquarium. They can live in a simple fish bowl like this.

Siamese Fighting Fish

Meet one of the toughest fish on the planet. For such a little guy, the *Betta splendens*, or Siamese fighting fish, as it's often called, is one feisty fish. Two males can't even be kept together because they'd fight to the finish—that is, until one is dead. Harsh! They were named for the country they come from, Siam, which today is known as Thailand.

Marvelous Males

The male *Betta*, with its long fins and deep colors, is easily one of the most beautiful fish you can own. The *Betta* comes in fantastic color combinations, like deep blue to purple, "watermelon" (green with red on the fins), and red. Sorry, girls, the females' colors are rarely as intense, nor are their fins as large, but the female *is* pretty—in a less showy way.

Put 'Em Up!

You can see the *Betta*'s fighting behavior without sacrificing a life. Hold a mirror up to the tank. A male *Betta* will see his reflection as another male in his territory and flare his gill covers and stick his fins straight up—the old "make him think I'm bigger than I am" routine.

Not all *Bettas* need to live apart, though. Three or more females can live peacefully together. Keeping two females together is not a good idea, though—one fish will probably bully the other. But there are divided *Betta* tanks, which allow you to keep two *Bettas* in the same tank, each separated from the other.

Betta Basics

One of the best things about *Bettas* is that they're relatively easy to care for. You might see *Bettas* kept in small bowls, but for optimum health and color, keep your *Betta* in a 3-gallon (10-liter) or larger tank. Plants improve water quality and provide hiding places, which help to cut down on aggression.

Bettas are surface eaters—they feed at the surface of the water. In the wild, they eat tiny sea animals and mosquito larvae (immature mosquitoes). Sprinkle *Betta* pellets—shrimp meal, bloodworms, and vitamins—on the water.

Betta Get One!

Betta splendens has much to recommend it as a pet. Few other fish are as beautiful, graceful, and easy to care for. But if you'd prefer an aquarium with many different fish living in harmony, this is not the choice for you!

Pieces of coral like this are often used as aquarium decorations.

Due to their fighting, Betta splendens *live in their own private aquariums. This small bowl is not the right size for a fish to live in all the time—it's just for display in a pet store.*

Frogs

Frogs have long been useful to people. They were good eating for Native Americans centuries ago. South American hunters even used the venom from the skin of poisonous frogs to make their arrows more deadly. There is no record of the first pet frog, but it's a safe bet that a kid exploring nature brought one home and asked, "Can I keep it?"

Tree Frog Basics

A White's tree frog is a popular pet frog. White's tree frogs live in trees in the wild, so their terrarium should be a good imitation of a tree. For one thing, it should be tall instead of long. Add tall plants (fake or real) and branches. Since tree frogs normally live in a moist climate, you'll need to spray the terrarium with bottled water. All frogs absorb moisture through their skin, so they're especially sensitive to chemicals in water.

Squawk!

White's tree frogs make a call that sounds like a loud repeating squawk. Males call to attract mates or to establish their territory. The only call that might come out of a female is a distress call in reaction to unwanted attention (if they don't like the way they're being handled or if they're sat on by a tank mate!).

The Chub Club

White's tree frogs are sometimes called dumpy frogs because they tend to get pretty chubby. In fact, they can overeat to the point where the fatty folds on the sides of the head grow over their eyes, leaving them unable to see. That means it's really important not to overfeed your frog.

Like most kinds of frogs, White's tree frogs eat crickets, and it's important to feed them only what they need, depending on their size and age. The best rule of thumb is to give them crickets that are no longer than the frog's head is wide. You can also offer adult frogs "pinkies"—newborn mice with no fur—once a week.

More Than Just a Pretty Face

White's tree frogs tend to change color, perhaps in response to temperature or humidity. They can be brownish, but most of the time they're green or blue-green.

The best thing about them is that once they are used to their new home, they're very easy to handle. They're just not particularly active—another reason they tend to get chubby! But if you're content to look at your pet, hold it, and care for it, a frog would love to have you for its friend.

A frog's terrarium should be filled with plants. The plants can be fake (like the ones shown here) or real. The only catch with real plants is that they need to be free of chemicals and pesticides.

White's tree frogs will sometimes sit atop one another. No one seems to know why. The top frog might be trying to establish dominance—that might explain why the frog being sat upon sometimes protests with a loud distress call. It's also possible that they like sitting on one other because they're soft and comfortable!

Turtles

Back in the 1960s, it was common for families to bring home a 1½-inch (4-centimeter) turtle in a plastic dish with a tiny plastic palm tree in the middle. Those turtles were red-eared sliders, which grow to 8–12 inches (20–30 centimeters) in length, so they outgrew their small enclosures in no time—and usually died prematurely. Fortunately, much more is known about caring for turtles now.

Fun in the Sun (and Water)

Red-eared sliders are semi-aquatic (they spend part of their time in the water). They thrive in warmer climates with warm, fresh, slow-moving water—you'll find them in ponds, on lakes, in marshes, and alongside creeks and streams. They love to bask in the sun, often piling up on logs or rocks in sunny areas. It's common to see four or five piled on top of each other.

Male sliders are usually smaller than the females and have longer tails and front claws. A male will swim backward in front of the female and wave his long claws at her to try to entice her to mate.

Room to Grow

Because a red-eared slider can grow to the size of a dinner plate, it will eventually need a very large tank. An adult turtle needs a tank almost as big as a bathtub! Two turtles need an even bigger tank.

When not in the water, pet turtles love to hang out on top of half logs.

Besides water to swim in, your slider will need a dry area for sunning and sleeping. This can be a floating cork raft or log, or you can make a beach at one end of the tank with aquarium gravel.

Turtle Tending

Your turtle's water will need to be partially drained and replaced with fresh warm water at least once a week and changed completely once a month.

Food consists of 25 percent or less live animals (little fish or earthworms from a pet shop), 25 percent or less commercial food (reptile pellets or tablets), and 50 percent or more live plant matter, like collard, mustard, and dandelion greens.

Is a Turtle for You?

Keeping a turtle involves quite a bit of work and requires a fair amount of space in your home. On the plus side, you can enjoy watching your turtle swim happily in its tank. You can give it greens to eat, and you can occasionally handle it. If that would make you smile, a turtle might be just the reptile for you!

Red-eared sliders are named for the patches of red on their heads (next to their eyes). The color is hard to see in this photo due to the color adjustments made to 3-D images, but you can see the color clearly if you look at the photo on page 61.

Leopard Geckos

The scientific name of the leopard gecko, *Eublepharis macularius*, says a lot about it. *Eublepharis* means "good (or true) eyelid," meaning an eyelid that covers the eye, which all the geckos of this family have. (Geckos in other families can't blink or sleep with their eyes closed.) The species name *macularius* means "spotted" (like a leopard).

Hot Stuff

Found wild in India, Afghanistan, and Pakistan, leopard geckos are now bred in captivity for the pet trade. Because they are desert dwellers, they'll need a heated terrarium as well as a special lamp for basking (lying in the warmth of the light).

Geckos are more active at night than during the day—they're used to hunting in the cool desert evening. Sunbathing is about all they do during the day! This means your reptile friend is more likely to come alive after sundown.

Quick Release

If a predator catches a leopard gecko by the tail, the gecko's tail will break off! The wiggling tail distracts the predator while the rest of the lizard gets away. If you grab your pet by the tail, the tail may break off—so be careful not to handle your guy by the tail. If your gecko does lose its tail, it may grow back. Give your gecko extra food and keep it away from any other geckos while the new tail is growing.

Gecko Pad

Leopard geckos, unlike most other geckos, do not have sticky toe pads, so they do not climb walls. However, your leopard gecko will appreciate a terrarium that's furnished with low-lying sticks to climb on, to bask on, and to sleep under during the day.

A 20-gallon (75-liter) terrarium is big enough for three geckos. Have a water dish big enough for your gecko to bathe in. Since geckos tend to poop in the water, be ready to change the water every day. Soaking in water helps your gecko to shed, too. A growing gecko will shed about once per month, or even every three weeks.

Are You Good to Get a Gecko?

The leopard gecko is the best starter lizard around. Supply it with calcium-loaded chow, live crickets, mealworms, and fresh water. Geckos generally don't make much noise other than a squeak or a hiss when they're slightly stressed. They're the ultimate mellow fellows.

Mealworms are a popular snack for leopard geckos and other reptiles.

Each of these baby leopard geckos has a different pattern of bands or stripes. As leopard geckos get older, they lose their bands or stripes and develop spots. These geckos are dipping in their water dish.

Bearded Dragons

Bearded dragons are lizards from Australia, the land "down under." Sometimes called lizards of Oz, bearded dragons are now bred all over the world. The "beards" on these lizards are dewlaps (folds of loose skin) under the chin, which they blow up to look more threatening. Weirder still, the females are bearded too! The only difference is that the male's beard tends to get darker than the female's.

Who's the Boss?

Although solitary in the wild, bearded dragons, known as "beardies," do communicate. A male will challenge another male by bobbing his head rapidly and inflating his beard. Males will end up fighting each other, so they shouldn't be kept together. When a lady lizard's around, the rapid bobbing means "Hello, sweet thing!" A female will sometimes bob her head rapidly if she feels she has to assert her dominance over another female.

Just Tryin' to Get Along

Beardies also "wave" one arm, circling it slowly. Observed even in babies, arm waving is believed to mean "I don't want to fight" and is often accompanied by a slower kind of head bobbing. A younger, smaller male will wave to avoid a fight with a bigger beardie.

All these social cues go to show that if you're planning to keep more than one bearded dragon, it is best to keep two females that are about the same size. Since they are generally loners in the wild, bearded dragons really don't need a buddy.

Lizard Lounge

An adult bearded dragon needs at least 6 square feet (about 0.5 square meter) of floor space in its tank. Because a baby beardie can get lost in a large space, it's better off in a smaller tank, and elaborate decorations are better saved for a bigger beardie. All beardies love to climb, and babies especially like climbing trees, so a branch or even a treelike plant is a good addition.

Bearded dragons need very little water. A little misting every day gives them all they need.

Are You a Dragon Devotee?

For those who don't adore lizards, bearded dragons have a face only a mother could love. For lizard lovers, though, they're real cuties. Because they are diurnal (active during the day), it's easy for us humans to watch all their fun behaviors. If you're considering a lizard, that's one good reason to decide on a dragon.

This terrarium decoration (complete with fake cactus) features a shallow water dish that can't be tipped over. This helps make sure a beardie won't go thirsty.

Two bearded dragons bask in the sun. See the white spikes under their chins? That's the "beard" they're named for. The beard will get much bigger and darker when the dragon puffs it out.

Blue-Tongued Skinks

A skink sure looks like a snake, with its triangular head and hard-to-see legs, but it's 100 percent lizard. The name *skink* comes from the Latin *scincus* and the Greek *skinkos*, meaning "lizard." Originally from Australia, skinks are real favorites among lizard lovers because of their gentle personality.

Snake Act

Some scientists think skinks sometimes defend themselves by imitating the death adder, a poisonous snake. The skink and the death adder have similar coloring, and the skink's tiny, almost unnoticeable legs contribute to the illusion. In another very effective defense behavior, the skink puffs itself up, opens wide its bright pink mouth, and extends its long blue tongue. Most predators think, "Whoa! That's got to be poisonous!" and leave the skink alone.

It's all just a good act. Blue-tongued skinks are known to be easily tamed and handled. Owners rarely see a full defensive display. The tip of blue tongue that skinks typically have poking out of their mouth (hence their name) is a more common sight.

Skink Digs

Since the blue-tongued skink is a large, wide-ranging lizard, it needs a large tank, which should be lined with wood shavings. While skinks are ground dwelling by nature, some enjoy climbing on sticks and

Skinks enjoy having plenty of sticks and logs in their terrarium for climbing.

logs, so it's good to have a few climbing sticks in the tank.

A large shallow water dish will also be welcome. Blueys, as blue-tongued skinks are sometimes called, are not great swimmers, but they do love to lie in their water.

Being omnivorous, skinks eat fruit, vegetables, and canned dog or cat food, with the occasional worm or mouse for an extra treat. They can learn to take food from your hand and will come to the front of the tank to greet you when you visit them.

Skink Care

It's OK to pick up a skink, but you should never grab one by the tail because, like many lizards, a skink will drop its tail to escape! Skinks are large, heavy lizards, so it's very important to support your skink's whole body when you handle it so that it feels safe. Your skink will fit nicely along your forearm, like it's lying on a log.

Once your blue-tongue gets used to you, it'll be content to hang out with you on the couch watching television or even meet your friends!

The two skinks shown here are different sizes because one is a baby! Baby skinks are about 4 inches (10 centimeters) long at birth, but they quickly grow to full size and are ready to fend for themselves shortly after birth.

Rosy Boas

The rosy boa is a member of the boa family, which includes the world's biggest snakes, among them the boa constrictor and anacondas. Never fear, though—the rosy boa is one of the smallest members of the family, usually growing to no more than 3 feet (1 meter) in length. It's a gentle snake, one of only two kinds of boas found in the wild in North America.

Showing Stripes

The most striking identifying feature of the rosy boa is its three lengthwise stripes. The rosy boa comes in many color combinations, and not all of them are rosy! There are bright oranges, soft roses and grays, high-contrast blacks and grays, and more. All the subspecies are beautiful.

Boa Basics

Being adapted to a dry environment, rosy boas need relatively little water. Some owners give their boas water only every other week to keep the tank dry. A rosy needs a heated tank that provides a range of temperatures, with the warm end of the tank 85–90° Fahrenheit (30–32° Celsius) and the cool end 75–80° Fahrenheit (24–27° Celsius).

Eat, Grow, Shed

Like other snakes, rosy boas eat mainly mice. Probably the most fun part of feeding your boa is

This "snake cave" offers a snake a cool and dark place to relax.

watching how it takes even a defrosted mouse with a quick strike and then constricts it—the rosy will wrap itself around its prey and squeeze it before swallowing it whole.

When your rosy boa's grown big enough, it'll put on the coolest show. It will shed its skin in one long piece that looks like a peeled-off stocking.

Smell Ya Later!

A rosy will often rest curled up in a ball with its head buried in the middle. In the wild, this position protects the snake from predators. When threatened, a rosy releases a foul smell from glands near the base of its tail. If your rosy stinks on you, it probably wants to be left alone.

Should You Bring Home a Snake?

That depends. You may have trouble persuading family members to allow a snake in your home, especially since your rosy will do best if it's handled regularly, and regular handling means out-of-tank time. As long as you're willing to do the work to keep your rosy warm, dry, and fed, you could have a companion for as long as 18 to 22 years!

In the wild, rosy boas will spend much of their time among rocks (especially in the heat of a summer day). They also enjoy climbing in low shrubs, so a branch is a good addition to the tank.

Corn Snakes

Does a corn snake eat corn? Early American settlers wondered because they so often found these snakes in their cornfields. They soon figured out that the snakes, instead of raiding the corn, were doing them a favor: They were eating the rats and other rodents that ate the corn! The beautiful corn snake is also gentle and easy to handle. It's considered one of the best snakes for a beginner.

Colorful Snake

Corn snakes come in many different colors and patterns, particularly shades of red, orange, and gray. There are even some white corn snakes.

Being crepuscular (mainly active at dusk and dawn), early morning and early evening are good times to handle a pet corn snake.

Corn Condo

Corns grow to be as long as 6 feet (2 meters), making a 20-gallon (75-liter) tank a must. Snakes are escape artists. Your enclosure should have a latch to keep the lid shut.

A heater at one end of the tank will give your corn a place to warm up. An inexpensive stick-on thermometer will help you monitor the temperature. A basking lamp is a plus, and a timer to turn it off and on is handy.

All snakes should have two "hides," one on the tank's cool side and one on the warm side. If there's a hide on only one side, a shy snake may toast or chill itself trying to stay hidden! Corns also love to climb, so add a branch. But beware: A corn will use the branch as an escape route first chance it gets, so keep that lid latched!

Feed Me!

One task that takes getting used to is feeding your pet snake prey. That means mice. The good news: The mice you feed your corn will be frozen. Young snakes eat "pinkies"—newborn mice with no fur—while older snakes feed on bigger mice or baby rats. Using tongs protects you from accidental bites. Watch as your corn "tastes" the air with its flicking tongue, sensing the meal to come, and then strikes.

It's important to feed the snake in a "feeding box," not its tank. If it's used to being fed in the tank, a snake may one day mistake your pinkie for the kind it gets at dinner!

Are You a Corn Companion?

If the thought of feeding mice doesn't turn you off and you think you'd like the feel of soft, leathery skin sliding across your hands, you may be an ideal companion for a corn snake.

This overturned coconut shell makes a great hide for a small snake.

Corn snakes come in many different "morphs" or combinations of color and pattern. This beauty has a vibrant orange body with brown spots that are ringed with black.

Tarantulas

Scary as it looks, a tarantula is one of the most fascinating creatures you can own. There are over 800 known species of tarantulas, found in warm areas all over the world. Most pet tarantulas are females, because females live much longer than the males—some for more than 20 years!

Fangs for the Memories

Tarantulas have venomous fangs with which they subdue their prey in the wild. While not known to be deadly to humans, a tarantula bite can be painful. Add to that the fact that tarantulas are delicate creatures and may die from a fall, and you can see why a tarantula should be handled very little, if at all.

Unlike many other spiders, tarantulas don't spin webs in which to capture their prey, but they do produce silk to create nests or line their burrows.

Crickets are the most common food for a tarantula. An adult tarantula will usually be satisfied with four crickets a week. As a rule, a tarantula can eat anything that is half its length or less.

Small World

A tarantula's cage should be small so that it can find its prey easily (tarantulas don't see too well). Adults can live happily in a lidded 5-gallon (20-liter) tank that is kept warm and humid. The lid is very important, as tarantulas can crawl straight up walls thanks to a sticky substance that oozes out of their feet.

Scary and Hairy

Tarantulas' bodies are covered with thousands of fine hairs. Most tarantulas have poor eyesight and use these hairs (called setae) to sense vibrations, find their prey, and even "taste" food.

Some species of tarantulas also have barbed (urticating) hairs, which can be released as a defense. These little hairs will irritate the eyes, skin, or nose of a predator—or anyone who gets too close.

New Skin? No Problem!

Being invertebrates (animals without backbones), tarantulas are protected by a strong exoskeleton (exterior skeleton). As the spider grows, its exoskeleton splits and the new, bigger spider sheds its "skin," a process called molting. When a tarantula molts, the "molt" (the shed exoskeleton) comes off in one piece, complete with fangs! Watching your tarantula molt is a great way to study its anatomy without risking injury to yourself or your spider. Tarantulas will not eat before molting—adults may go without food for as long as several weeks. The spider is very vulnerable while molting and can be killed even by a cricket. It can be 1 week to 10 days before an adult's new exoskeleton dries and the creature is able to eat again.

So, Is a Tarantula for You?

Being a spider wrangler isn't too tough a gig. If you are willing to look but not touch and keep your spider warm, moist, and fed, you might have this thrilling, chilling companion for a long time to come!

These are Chilean rose hair tarantulas, one of the most common types of pet tarantula. Tarantulas can handle the heat—in the wild, they live in hot climates, such as those of South America and the southwestern United States.

More Fun with 3-D

A 3-D image that you view with red and blue glasses is called an *anaglyph*. Anaglyph images lose some of their natural colors when the right and left eye images are converted to red and blue (see page 11). Another kind of 3-D image is a "stereo pair." When you look at a stereo pair using the method described below, you'll see a 3-D image that has all its true colors.

The stereo pairs shown here are small, which makes them fairly easy to view. They should be clear and colorful.

Tube View

Roll up two sheets of letter-size paper the long way. Then hold one tube above the left-eye image and one above the right-eye image. The effect is like looking through binoculars. Relax your eyes and let them almost cross. The two images will slide toward each other and meet as a single 3-D image in the middle. Tube viewing takes a little practice, but it's exciting when you make it happen.

| *Left Eye* | *Right Eye* | *Left Eye* | *Right Eye* |

| *Left Eye* | *Right Eye* | *Left Eye* | *Right Eye* |

Left Eye *Right Eye* *Left Eye* *Right Eye*

Left Eye *Right Eye* *Left Eye* *Right Eye*

Left Eye *Right Eye* *Left Eye* *Right Eye*

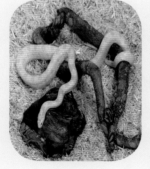

Left Eye *Right Eye* *Left Eye* *Right Eye*

61